THE DORSET COAST
Photographs by Bob Croxford

From Lyme Regis to Mudeford the coast of Dorset is rich in variety. Cliffs, coves, harbours and holiday resorts all exist in a splendid mixture. Most of the coastline is now part of the World Heritage Jurassic Coast.

This small book starts at the east of the county and follows the coast westwards to Lyme Regis.

Published by Atmosphere
Willis Vean
Mullion Cornwall TR12 7DF
England
Tel 01326 240 180
email info@atmosphere.co.uk

ISBN 0 9543409 0 6

Printed and bound in Italy

Cover: Man O'War Bay

Frontispiece: Crab pots at Mudeford

Crabber off Durlston Head

Hengistbury from Mudeford

Christchurch

Brownsea Island

Brownsea Island

The Old Customs House, Poole

Poole Waterfront

Poole Harbour. Fishing boats and sailing boats

Bournemouth

Sandbanks - Studland Ferry

Studland Dunes

Studland Bay

Old Harry Rocks

Handfast Point & The Pinnacles

Swanage

Dancing Ledge

Coast looking toward St Adhelm's Head

Clavel's Tower, Kimmeridge

Kimmeridge, old harbour wall

Lulworth Cove

Durdle Door

Lulworth Cove

Durdle Door

Man O' War Bay

PETITE ANGELA

Weymouth Harbour

Weymouth Harbour

Weymouth Harbour

42

Weymouth Harbour at dusk

Portland Bill, Pulpit Rock

Portland Bill Lighthouse

Sunset on the Fleet from Portland

St. Catherine's Chapel above Abbotsbury with the Fleet beyond

Cogdon Beach   *Flowers on the shingle at Cogden Beach*   51

Jurassic Cliffs at Bridport

West Bay Harbour

Ammonite

Golden Cap

Golden Cap

The Cobb at Lyme Regis

The Cobb and harbour at Lyme Regis

Lyme Regis

Fishing boat in Lyme Bay

INDEX

Endpiece: Dawn at Studland Beach